Profiting in Precious Metals

Profiting in Precious Metals

Copyright © 2014 Ron Cowart

All Rights Reserved

No part of this book may be reproduced, stored or transmitted by any means, without express written permission by the publisher.

KNIGHTYME PRODUCTIONS

Published by Knightyme Productions, Zachary, Louisiana

ISBN-13: 978-1494919856
ISBN-10: 1494919850

Profiting in Precious Metals

Table of Contents

Introduction

Chapter 1 – Tools of the Trade

Chapter 2 – Gold

How to determine what is real and what is not

Some rules of thumb

Items to NOT purchase

Chapter 3 – Silver

Sterling silver

Silver coins

Chapter 4 – Platinum

Chapter 5 – Testing

The test

White Metal

Stannous Chloride Recipe

Chapter 6 – Buying

Items to purchase

Items to NOT purchase

Chapter 7 – Selling

Chapter 8 – Glossary

Chapter 9 – Resources

Chapter 10 – In Closing

Free gifts

About the Author

Profiting in Precious Metals

Introduction

In 1993, a close friend of mine, who at the time owned and operated a mid-sized jewelry store, 'took me under his wing' and taught me the finer details of his trade. In the process of doing so, he taught me how he made 'extra money', that is, how he added income on top of his regular sales of wedding bands, necklaces, earrings, etc.. This added income was generated from his purchase of *scrap* gold, silver and platinum. Needless to say, I was surprised, if not taken slightly aback, at the amount he was able to buy within a week's time, not to mention what he ended up making off of it in the end.

My friend ended up selling his store shortly after losing his wife to illness. He moved out of town, and we eventually lost contact with each other, as we went our separate ways. While it's a shame we did lose touch with each other, the things he taught me, the *tricks of his trade*, if you will, never left me. In fact, the one subject that stuck with me, eventually led me to begin buying my own scrap metal. Of course, since I didn't own a store to which the sellers of such scrap could come to me, I was forced to improvise. I tried different methods of locating old rings, dental gold and the likes, some of which were successful while others failed to produce.

While I have retired, the methods in this book work as well as when I first published this book, in electronic format (e-book) back in 2005. Prior to publishing the e-book version, I had never shared this information with anyone. Now that I have, one of your questions may be "won't the market get saturated?" The short answer to your question is "no, absolutely not." The more detailed answer is "it's impossible for the market to become saturated, as there really are fewer 'doers' (people who will actually pursue this business) than procrastinators. And the scrap that becomes available for purchase does so on a daily basis."

I hope that you enjoy what you read through-out this book, and more importantly, I hope that you find it beneficial in adding to your own little 'nest egg'. In reading the information contained herein, remember that your future purchases won't be for the anesthetic value of a ring or pin, and it won't have a thing to do with the fact that an article belonged to

Profiting in Precious Metals

the great-grandmother of a past Governor. It will be simply for the content of the precious metal which that article contains.

One Man's Trash is Another Man's Treasure

Even during slow economic times, precious metals tend to hold their market value. While others are holding their collective breaths, watching as the stock markets roller-coaster their investments, holders of precious metals keep plodding on, adding to their stock or selling to go on vacation.

How does one go about investing in precious metals? Futures, perhaps? While futures or commodities are certainly one way to consider, and many investors have done well with them, they're not for everyone. The learning curve can be steep, and depending on how gutsy one is, it can be a costly learning curve as well. This reference explores *other* ways to invest in precious metals, and hopefully, having fun while doing so. This reference targets the average investor, the one who works 40+ hours a week, and brings just enough home to make ends meet.....sometimes.

Consider the *scrap* metal around you. Can you think of any, that contain any one of the three precious metals, that have already been mentioned? What's that? A ring that nobody wears any longer? And what is that stamped into the inner portion of the ring? 14K you say? Hmmmmmm...is that worth anything? And you saved your old gold filling from that trip to your dentist. Why did you save it? Did your dentist tell you to? Or is it because, you knew, instinctively, that it was worth something still, even though it was no longer used for it's original purpose? These, and literally hundreds of other items, are all around us, at almost any given time. Forgotten rings, watches, fillings, crowns, pins, medals, and the list goes on, most containing one of the three metals you now seek, are available to you. All you need to know, is where to look, whom to ask, and what to say and pay.

So, if you're interested in buying and selling precious metals, by all means, continue on. Those who make a living in this business are few, meaning that your competition is virtually non-existent. Did I say "make a living?" You bet I did. In fact, depending on your self-motivation, and

Profiting in Precious Metals

this pertains to any self-run business, you can parlay this business into financial independence, in a relatively short time. As in any business, you need tools, knowledge, a goal, and perhaps most importantly, *desire*. The good news is, you evidently have most of what it takes to make it in this business! How do I know that? As I previously stated, desire is a key requirement. If you did not possess the desire to succeed, I really feel that you would not be reading this now. With the desire to succeed, it's almost inevitable that you have set a goal of where you want to be at a particular time in your life. If you haven't done that, now is a good time. Set a goal, and make it a reasonable goal, of where you want to be financially, say one year from now. Then, three years from now, and ten years from now. Write those goals down, and put them away (where you can readily access them to see if you're 'on target'). And you need the knowledge and tools. You're gaining knowledge right now, this very minute. And as for the tools, read on.

In this reference you will learn what tools you will need, how to recognize an 'investment' versus a 'plated collectible'. You'll learn what to buy, when to buy and how to determine what you should pay. You will become familiar with terms that are commonplace among the flea market devotees and estate buyers. Most importantly though, once you complete this reference, you will have learned how to *not* worry when the economy begins to stall, and the stock market's negative closings seem to permeate the news over everything else. You will be in a position to do well in bad economic times, and to excel in the best of economic times. You will be effectively 'depression-proof'. You will be able to *put your hands on* your investment, anytime you desire. And you will be able to sell your investment, anytime you desire.

Sound exciting? Excellent! Prepare yourself for a rewarding, even fun future, in this relatively little-known 'mom and pop' business.

Profiting in Precious Metals

Chapter 1

Tools of the Trade

Now that you have decided that investing in precious metals is for you, it's time to consider some of the 'tools of the trade'. All of the tools listed below are available at one or more of the sites listed under 'Resources.'

Gold Test Kit

Once you become active in buying precious metals, this kit will become one of your 'best friends'. It contains *nitric acid* which you will learn to use, to verify that you are indeed buying gold, test needles (to assist in determining karat value) and a test stone (more on this in the testing section).

Profiting in Precious Metals

Electronic Gold Tester

If the idea of using acid is what keeps you away from this business, then by all means, don't use it. That's where the electronic gold tester comes in. They are widely available, and I'm told they're also highly accurate. I used nitric acid before I retired, so I cannot speak from experience.

Profiting in Precious Metals

Safety Glasses

Your gold test kit may come first but if you decided to use the acid test kit, your personal safety should be considered next. These are the type of glasses I prefer (no strap) but there are precious metal buyers who use nothing but their regular, everyday eyeglasses. It's your eyes and therefore, your call.

Safety Gloves

Make sure the gloves are certified to stand up to use with acid and similar corrosive chemicals.

Profiting in Precious Metals

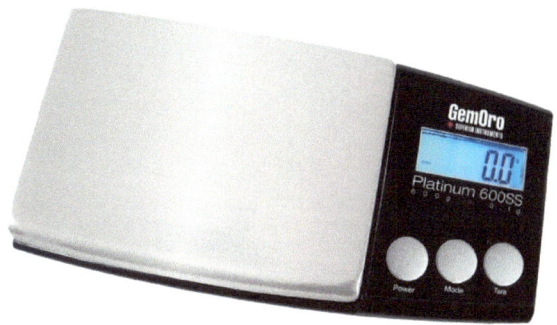

Gold Scale

You can purchase these locally or online. Beginners should consider sticking to the digital pocket scales, as they are accurate and highly portable. The one thing you need to remember when purchasing a gold scale is to make certain it weighs in DWT (pennyweight).

Jewelers Loupe

I used carry one of these to get a little 'closer look at things'. Indistinguishable karat marks, test marks on stones, etc.. They're worth every bit of the relatively small amount they cost.

Profiting in Precious Metals

Triangular File

This file should not exceed 6" in length (portability is everything) and can be found at any hardware store. Remember, you will use the sharp edge or corner to carve out a relatively deep notch in the item to be tested.

Small Magnet

This little tool can be kept in your pocket or purse, and will no doubt prove itself to be handy. Small magnets, suitable for your needs, can be found at hobby shop and/or hardware stores. **NOTE**: *Gold Plated* items will be drawn to a magnet. Real gold will not.

Profiting in Precious Metals

Needle Nose Pliers

These can be found in any hardware store and in most hobby shops. They will prove indispensable when handling small, delicate items and in removing articles, e.g., cameos, stones, etc., from items to be tested.

Workbench

Last but not least comes a workbench. I saved this for last as it's definitely not a necessity but falls in the ranks of *something you may wish to add later on*. The picture is one of a personal workbench which I personally used. I found that it comes in handy when 'going on location' to make a purchase and not having an optimum work area available. Also, it served to keep me from accidently damaging a seller's furniture! This one was purchased off of eBay for just a few dollars.

Profiting in Precious Metals

Chapter 2

Gold

Gold is going to be one of your best money makers, and as such, you will note that this chapter is a little 'meatier' than those pertaining to silver and platinum.

How to Determine What is Real and What is Not

We have all heard of 10K, 14K, 24K, etc. gold before. And most of us know that the 'K' stands for 'KARAT' or the *karat weight* of gold. But what is karat? What does the word karat signify?

Karat is the term used to specify what portion of the alloy, that makes up a piece of jewelry, etc. is *pure* gold. Think about that for just a moment. If that's what karat denotes, then it would be accurate to say that the karat weight of pure gold is 24K. By the same token, something that is only part gold, and 10 parts of another metal, would be 14K gold.

It's really pretty simple isn't it? And that simplicity is part of the beauty of this business. Once you get the hang of locating, testing, buying and selling, you'll really enjoy the freedom this business affords one. Anyway, back to the lesson.

In the business of buying scrap gold, silver, etc. you'll soon see that the vast majority of the scrap gold you pick up will be in the 10K to 14K range. 18K has picked up in popularity but the overall majority will fall within the lesser figures. Yellow dental gold will be approximately 16K. Dental gold, however, will **not be stamped**. Just remember that the higher the karat weight, the **more pure gold** and **less other alloy** is present in a given item.

Some 'Rules of Thumb'
Items To Purchase
Any items stamped with the following numbers...

- 10K

Profiting in Precious Metals

- 12K
- 14K
- 18K

You will want to consider, and therefore, test for gold content, the following items, as well...

- **Rings** - whenever you advertise the fact that you buy scrap metal (covered in detail later), do yourself a favor and don't forget to list 'rings' among the list of things you buy. They are in abundance, from engagement rings missing stones (or those who wore them), to tongue rings, typically originating from those who outgrew them. Regardless of the type of ring, this item will prove to be a moneymaker for you.
- **Watches** - are another excellent item to consider when running your ads. Wrist watches and pocket watches are the two types you want to concern yourself with. And don't forget the metal watchbands. Some people save them, with the intention of placing it on another watch sometime in the future, only that day seems to never arrive. So much the better for you. You'll not want to skip the testing here. Many of these bands will prove to be plated but you will run across enough that are the real thing, to make it worth your while.
- **Medals, Awards, Trophies** - you will run across a *ton* of these, especially if you frequent estate sales. Such items may have been coveted by those who received them but you'll find that those who sell them, think considerably less of them. Medals will prove to be the ones you buy most often but trophies, in particular those that originated from top corporations, can prove to be a 'diamond in the rough'.
- **Cuff Links** - you will find these in flea markets, estate sales, and individuals answering your 'Scrap Metal Wanted' ads. They're small in size but, unlike rings, they typically come in pairs. Another thing I like about this business is the fact that *small* packages can reap a *lot* of rewards!
- **Lodge Pins** - you will find that these are plentiful. Especially in estate sales, flea markets, etc., where it's not uncommon to find

them bulked in baskets or boxes, just waiting for you to pick through.
- **Yellow Dental Gold** - I'm convinced that the *mother lode* of dental gold, remains untouched. The good news is that it will always remain untouched. Think about it. People save it, and what do they do with it? They throw it in a jewelry box or other equally out of the way place, and forget about it. In fact, it may go forgotten for years, until they read your ad saying that you buy scrap metal, including *dental gold*. **NOTE**: Throughout this book, whenever I mention dental gold, I inevitably specify *yellow* dental gold. The reason for this is that white or silver colored dental gold can prove to be a pain to identify. Some of the white metals used by dentists are white gold or platinum-palladium alloys. I could go into further detail here and tell you why, and how these different metals can deceive you into thinking they're gold, but I won't. Suffice it to say that I personally stick to yellow dental gold and recommend that you do the same.

Items To **NOT** Purchase

Any items marked with the following...

- **G.F** - means that the item is gold-filled. For your purposes, stay away from it.
- **R.G.P.** - means the item is 'Rolled Gold Plate'. Keep your money in your pocket.
- **H.G.E.** - Heavy Gold Electroplate (need I say more?)
- **10K G.F., 14K G.F., etc.** - and a myriad of additional variations. If it doesn't say what you're looking to buy...then leave it alone.

Don't let any of the above overwhelm you. And by all means, don't try to commit every last detail to memory. It's just not necessary. If you approach this business in a simple way, you will find that it really is simple. In time, you will find that you have totally discarded all of your little detailed 'cheat sheets' (well, maybe not all of them) and your confidence level will soar.

Profiting in Precious Metals

If you fail to remember everything else you learn here, then do yourself a favor and do remember this. Remembering this one thing will get you out of a jam that you may not even realize you've worked your way into, and it will certainly save you some grief when it comes to your bank account.

WHEN IN DOUBT....<u>TEST!</u>

Profiting in Precious Metals

Chapter 3

Silver

Silver, as you may have already surmised, will most likely be next in line (behind gold) as your biggest source of income. You will enjoy many opportunities to make profitable silver purchases, all the way from silver coins and bullion to silver commemorative medals and the like. Silver, like gold, is non-magnetic and is only about one-half as heavy as gold.

Sterling Silver

You have no doubt seen the word *Sterling* before, marked on a ring or other item of high silver content. While it may not have meant much to you in the past, you should now look at it from a totally different perspective, that is if you are reading this material to profit from it!

The *Sterling* mark designates that the item on which you see the mark is 92.5 percent pure silver and 7.5 percent copper. Since silver, in it's pure state, is too soft for ordinary use, copper is added to give it strength.

When you see the *Sterling* stamp or mark, you can assume that the item originated in the USA. While I won't say that you will never see the same mark or stamp used on an item from the UK, it is indeed rare when you do. Items made in the UK which are slated from export, may very well, and in all likelihood, bear the *Sterling* mark.

Silver Coins

Silver coins are comprised of 90% silver and 10% copper. You'll note a slight difference in the percentages of composition between the coins and sterling items. The reason for this slight difference (2.5% more copper in the coins) is the improvement of wearing qualities. Even though this additional copper inclusion does indeed improve the wearing qualities of the coins, it does not detract from the silver appearance. In fact, the difference in copper between silver coins and

Profiting in Precious Metals

that of sterling is so minute that even experienced handlers often find it difficult to distinguish between the two.

At this point you may very well be asking yourself how one goes about determining what is sterling, etc.. For your answer to that question as well as all 'precious metal testing' questions, refer to the chapter on 'Testing.'

Composition of Silver Alloys			
The Alloy	**Mark**	**Fine Silver**	**Alloy**
Fine or Pure Silver (bars or ingots)	.999+	99.9+%	Trace
Britannia Silver (highest grade used in UK)	Hallmark Figure (Lady Britannia) Player Name	95.84%	4.16%
Sterling Silver	Sterling	92.5%	7.5%
Coin	Coin/Coin Silver	90%	10%
Low Quality European Silver	.800	80%	20%
NOTE: The above table does not cover ALL items but should serve as a guide to 90%+ items.			

Profiting in Precious Metals

Chapter 4

Platinum

Even though gold and silver (in that order) will no doubt prove to be your moneymakers (they were mine as well), I decided to include platinum for two reasons. First, it was included in my 'tutorial' when my jewelry store friend told me how to make money in this business. And second, because you may very well run across a platinum wedding set or two that you will have the opportunity to purchase for scrap. Granted, I can count on one hand the number of times I've been offered platinum but that's me and my area. I can't begin to believe that every other place in the world would prove to be as 'dry'.

Platinum Wedding Bands

This chapter on platinum will be rather short, at least when compared to the others on gold and silver. The reason being is that there isn't a lot to be said about this precious metal. It can easily be mistaken for white-gold but if you, like me, limit yourself to buying only those items which are marked with an accepted mark, e.g., *Platinum* or *Pt.*, then you really know about as much as you need to in order to make money.

Platinum is the rarest of the 'big 3' (my terminology) precious metals. That is one of the reasons you don't see platinum being touted as a measure of wealth in ancient times, like you see gold and even silver.

Profiting in Precious Metals

Large deposits of the metal were discovered, by accident, when the Spanish were looking for gold during the 16th century conquest of South America. In fact, the Spaniards named the new metal after the river, from which it was discovered, the Rio-Pinto (platina del pinto).

Platinum can be found as nuggets in alluvial sands in the Urals, California, South America and Mexico. Interestingly enough, platinum is also recovered as a by-product in a number of metallurgical operations in the production of copper, nickel, lead, etc..

Platinum is a heavy, tenacious, steel-gray metal that assumes it's silver-white appearance (the appearance we are familiar with) after being refined. While platinum can weather moist air and any single common acid, it will dissolve readily in aqua regia. Platinum will typically be alloyed with silver (66% silver to 33% platinum) in goldsmith's work. This combination is referred to as *platinum silver* and the resulting product can be polished.

Well, I told you this would be a brief chapter. Just remember to refer to the chapter on testing if you wish to test an item that isn't marked. Or feel free to follow my KISS method and avoid the extra confusion. Either way, you should know enough now to make money with it (you know as much as I do).

Profiting in Precious Metals

Chapter 5

Testing

This is where your *Gold Test Kit* becomes your 'best friend'. If you have not yet obtained one, now would be an ideal time.. Telling the difference between real gold, and that which is not real gold, can make you or break you in this business. Fortunately, the science of telling that difference isn't 'rocket science'.

The best method for testing both gold and silver, is with nitric acid. Using a gold test kit, like the one shown below, can make the process easy and safe.

Before we get into the details of how you actually conduct the test, it's time for a little disclaimer.

Nitric acid is <u>very poisonous</u> and it is a corrosive liquid that <u>should be handled with extreme care</u>, at all times! When working with this acid, it is recommended that you wear glasses or safety glasses, to protect your eyes. Any contact with the skin will result in a burning sensation, and that area which is affected should be flushed with water, as soon as possible.

Profiting in Precious Metals

Gee whiz Ron, why on earth would I want to get involved with any business that could prove to be as dangerous as this one sounds? Well, for starters....the tremendous profits that are truly available! As for the *danger*, I certainly won't pretend that the potential for danger isn't present. However, to date, I've not been even slightly 'stung' by handling the nitric acid and provided you take the proper precautions, you won't be either. Like anything else, let your common sense be the judge. You'll soon find that opening a champagne bottle can prove to be equally as hazardous.

The Test

To determine if a gold colored article is real gold or not, you should first clean the surface of the article to be tested. If the article has any *coating*, e.g., transparent varnish, lacquer, plastic, etc., this needs to come off. You are seeking the surface of the article. Anything less and the test will be anything but accurate.

When you are certain that you're down to the true surface, put a single drop of nitric acid on the area to be tested. Gold that is high in actual gold content, e.g., 14K, 16K, 18K and on up to 24K, **will show no change.**

On the other hand, when you get down to the lower karat gold's, you will then begin to see a reaction to the acid. For example, gold that is 12K will show a very slight change. Gold that is 10K or less, will change to a brown color on the spot where you applied your drop of acid. In other words, the less reaction to the acid, the more gold present. If the metal which you are testing is yellow, and it shows no reaction to the nitric acid, you can rest comfortably knowing that you are dealing with a gold alloy. **There is no other yellow metal (that I know of) that will show no reaction to nitric acid**.

One of the best ways to learn to test gold, is to test articles of *known content*. For instance, if you have a ring or watch band which you know is 14K gold, test it to see the results. The more articles, with varying degrees of content you can test, which have a known content to you, the better. It's kind of like rehearsing for a play. The better you are with

Profiting in Precious Metals

your lines and positioning, the more confidence you will have. And the more confidence you possess, the more professional you appear and the less likely that anyone will try to put something over on you.

Determining the Karat of Gold

Determining the karat of gold is not essential to being a success in buying precious metals for a profit. However, I feel like it's one of those 'things you may want to know' in the future, for a myriad of reasons. One of those reasons could be as simple as impressing a potential seller, who has stated that they don't know the karat of the item you're interested in buying. When you demonstrate that you can accurately determine the, *approximate* karat value of the item, they come to realize that you're there to do business and are more likely to accept your first offer as opposed to bartering. How you end up using this information (or not for that matter) is entirely up to you. I learned it and even though I came to realize it's not a requirement, I feel obligated to provide you with the same opportunity.

Step 1

Take the item to be tested and drag it lightly across the test stone (included in your gold test kit). How lightly do you drag it? Light enough so that no mark is left on the item itself but heavy enough so that a faint 'gold streak' is left along the path you dragged the item on the test stone. I really came to appreciate this testing method simply because it doesn't require any acid being administered directly to the test item.

Step 2

Select the gold test needle that closest matches the karat mark or what your estimate of the karat to be. For example, if you wish to confirm an item to be 14 karat, begin with the 14 karat needle. Then lightly drag the needle (the same way you did with the test item) across the stone and across your previous mark (from the test item), so that you are now looking at a gold 'X' on the stone.

Profiting in Precious Metals

Step 3

Finally, apply a small amount of test solution that matches the karat of your test needle. For example, 14 karat needle, use the 14 karat solution. Apply this solution to the middle of your 'X' mark or where the two lines you made cross. If both marks on the stone **remain**, then test item is **that karat or higher**. However, If the mark from the test item **dissolves**, the karat is **lower** than the karat number of the solution.

I realize that it's inevitable that some of you will end up investing in a solution for each and every karat. However, that is not necessary. Remember that one of the great advantages of this business is it's *portability*. If an item tests higher than 10 karat and lower than 14, it's 12 karat. Simple, uncomplicated and it packs light to boot! One other thing to remember is that this test should not be the only test, especially in determining if an item is solid gold. The above test only tells you about the surface of the item. If you suspect an item to be gold plated, then the more in-depth notch test should be completed.

It's fairly acceptable to assume that articles which are stamped with a karat mark really are of that quality. However, I encourage everyone who reads this book, to **test everything**! If you get into the habit of testing, early on, then the less likely you will suffer a loss in this business. Remember, one mismarked piece of gold can result in a significant loss, especially when one considers today's prices. So, do yourself a favor, and test. It pays dividends in the end.

White Metal

You will occasionally run across white metals that are offered to you as white gold. Since you are in the business of buying precious metals, you'll want to include white gold in your inventory, when the opportunity presents itself.

Just because the gold offered to you is not yellow, don't let it throw you. If the metal is white, and it's stamped with a karat value, you can be about 99.99% certain that it's legitimate. On the other hand, if it's not marked with a karat value, and it shows no reaction to nitric acid, there is about the same chance that it is one of several potential alloys (other than gold) which do not show a change with nitric acid. Some of the alloys are platinum, palladium, stainless steel, and the list goes on. What is relevant to you is the fact that it's not gold.

With that said, how does one determine if an article is indeed white gold? Prior to learning how to test white gold, it's important that you understand why it is white to begin with. White gold alloys contain the same percentages of gold, per karat, as the yellow gold alloys. However, they also contain enough of some white metal to nullify the yellow color that we normally associate with gold. Why on earth would anyone want to purchase *white* gold, especially as an article of jewelry? I don't know, you'll have to ask those you buy from but I suspect that in some cases, it would be due to the fact that some people prefer the silver color, yet have allergic reactions to silver. Assuming that it's not karat stamped, you can use the same method as you did to test yellow gold, in order to verify white gold.

Silver - Solid Silver or Silver Plate?
When I wrote this, one of my foremost goals was to make it simple and easy to understand. The more simple it is, the more readily you will retain that which you read and hopefully will be that much more profitable since you're able to remember it easier. With that said, allow me to share with you my tired and true methodology of keeping it simple and quick!

For those items that I run across that are marked or stamped *Sterling*. I simply take them for face value. In other words, I accept the fact that they are sterling and pay accordingly. So far, I've not run across a single item that was so marked that proved to be a fake or reproduction. Why do you figure this is? Simple. The cost to reproduce something that is sterling would far outweigh that which you could expect to get back on it. It's just not worth the effort. I won't say that it will never happen.

However, I can and will say that I have not seen it. Below are just a few of the many different types of hallmarks one can expect to encounter.

Don't worry yourself with knowing all there is to know about the marks though. Unless you're just into that sort of thing, it would prove to be a serious waste of time and effort (better spent on locating items to buy!) for most of us. There are just too many marks out there and they can prove difficult to interpret. My suggestion is to leave the marks to the experts.

Solid Silver or Silver Plate?

A single drop of nitric acid on the surface of a silver colored item will quickly tell you if that item is silver or not. When nitric acid touches a silver item, it produces a dark spot. Then, when you wipe the spot, you will notice an obvious grey colored area around the spot. This simple test will tell you in a second or two if the surface of the item is silver or not.

If you suspect or have been informed by the seller that the item is solid silver, you will want to probe a little deeper. You will want to take your triangular file (see Tools) and, using the edge of the file, carve a notch in the surface of the item. This notch should be deep enough to get below the surface and expose the base metal below it. Then apply a drop of nitric acid to the notch you just made. If the item is indeed solid silver, the metal in the notch and the surface around the notch will turn gray in color. This is caused by the reaction of the metal to the nitric acid. If the item is silver *plated*, the area around the notch will turn gray. However, the metal below the surface, upon coming in contact with the nitric acid, will turn green in color!

Profiting in Precious Metals

A word of caution here. If the item you are considering for purchase is intended to be sold for scrap metal, a notch in the item won't mean a thing. On the other hand, if the item is a valuable piece which isn't considered to be scrap, then you may want to avoid the acid test. At this point, I've got to tell you that unless it's obvious scrap silver (which I don't mind notching), I don't consider it for purchase. Why? Well, generally speaking, if the item is *of value* for reasons other than it precious metal content, say for example, a family heirloom, then the seller is going to expect more money. And you've got to remember, this business is lucrative because you're not buying investments.....you are buying scrap.

A Final Word On Silver

We have learned that a small drop of nitric acid on the surface of a silver item will produce a gray spot. It's important to know that silver is the only such *white metal* that will produce such a reaction. Platinum, white gold and stainless steel will produce no reaction.

Most purchasers of precious metals (myself included), upon noting the presence of the *Sterling* mark on an item of interest, will accept that item as silver without testing. I've yet to lose money on this most reasonable assumption. You should proceed with what makes you comfortable.

The *Other* White Metal

After reading that *platinum, white gold and stainless steel will produce no reaction*, you may be wondering, and justifiably so, how does one determine if an item is platinum? Well, testing for platinum on the surface of an item is pretty straight-forward. And frankly, other references on this same subject will stop right there, at the surface. The reason being is that it can get a little tricky when determining if a test item is *solid* platinum.

If the gold test kit (acid test, not the electronic tester) you purchased contains the platinum solution, you're ready to test the surface of a

Profiting in Precious Metals

platinum item. If not, don't despair as the platinum solution can be purchased separately and thereby added to your kit. For the purpose of this tutorial, I will assume that you have one already.

Scratch the test item over your test stone, pressing with enough force so as to leave a large, think visible deposit. Drop some of the platinum test solution on the scratch you just made. If the material on the stone is platinum, it should retain it's white, bright color. Just that simple!

The platinum test solution can also be utilized for both 14k and 18k white gold. For 14k white gold, the material on the stone should disappear in about fifteen to twenty seconds. For 18k white gold, the material on the stone will change to a light bronze color. This process of changing color depends on a couple of different variables but should take place in anywhere from two to three minutes.

My friend elected to use the *stannous chloride test* in order to determine if an item is platinum. The advantage in using this test is that it will give you a conclusive answer as to if an item is solid platinum or not. The down side is that you will need to concoct the test solution yourself, and since it doesn't have a lengthy shelf life, you will probably need to do that for just about every item you consider purchasing. Do I use the stannous chloride test? No. In fact, I never have. I've never even made the solution. I have seen the solution made and the process does appear easy enough. My friend, who provided me with the recipe used it, largely I think, because he had the facilities right there (his jewelry store) and he had occasion to see much more platinum than I have (or will for that matter). I follow the KISS (Keep It Simple Son) method in that if someone offers me something they say is platinum...fine. If it bears a mark that says "*Platinum*" or "*Pt*", then I will buy it (provided the price is right). If the mark is not present, I pass. My point is this. I have not been offered enough platinum for purchase consideration to warrant my making the stannous chloride test solution even once! The platinum that I have been offered was marked properly anyway. However, for those of you who would like the recipe for the stannous chloride solution, click the link below. I want you to have the same option I did in either using it or passing on it.

Stannous Chloride Test Solution (recipe)

Ingredients

- stannous chloride crystals/powder
- one-half ounce acid testing bottle
- water
- hydrochloric acid
- aqua regia test solution

Making the Solution

Take about a pennyweight (or less) of the stannous chloride crystals/powder and dissolve it in the one-half ounce acid testing bottle, three-fourths full of water. Add to the stannous chloride/water solution about 25 drops of hydrochloric acid. The resulting milky-looking solution is your new 'test liquid' for platinum.

Testing for Platinum

Use the bottom of a small white porcelain saucer (white so that the results of your test, which produces colors, can be seen easily). Use a piece of emery cloth to rub a dull spot, on the glaze of the saucer, about the size of a U.S. fifty cent piece. Now rub the test metal on the roughened spot, making a heavy streak. Dissolve the mark with aqua regia test solution. Warm the saucer over an open light bulb for a few minutes (platinum tends to dissolve slowly when cold and faster when heated). If the acid evaporates, add another drop of aqua regia. Once the metallic streak (which you made by rubbing the metal on the spot you made) has dissolved, add a couple of drops of your stannous chloride solution. If the metal in the streak is indeed platinum, a deep yellow or brown color will form. If the streak is really rich in platinum, the color will turn almost black.

Tip: If you decide that you wish to pursue the stannous chloride solution as your preferred method of testing, then by all means go for it. In order

Profiting in Precious Metals

to lengthen the shelf life of the solution, you can add a small piece of pure tin to the solution. The piece of tin should not be any larger than a match head.

Profiting in Precious Metals

Chapter 6

Buying

Ok, you've got this far, so I'll assume that you want to make some money in this business. I'll further assume (just for progress) that you have obtained the tools you will need to conduct yourself as a professional buyer of precious metals. Now it's time to locate the *stuff*!

Fortunately, this is the easy part and it only gets easier as you become more established. In fact, before you realize it, people will be locating you....and 90% of those that do will do so via word-of-mouth (some of the BEST advertising there is in this business).

Bulk Mail
In my beginning days in this business, I had some inexpensive postcards printed up (see below) which I used to conduct direct mailings in my area. You may be wondering how I came up with names and addresses to which I could mail to. The fact of the matter is that the way I conducted my mass mailings was a virtual 'turkey shoot'. I used our local phone book and pulled out random names and addresses and mailed! Well, guess what? It worked! Not on a large scale but to a degree that it more than paid for my postcard investment! So, I did another mailing, only this time I doubled the amount I sent out. What was the result? I'll answer it like this. My tool investment was paid for, strictly on mail results and I still conduct periodic mailings (twice a year).

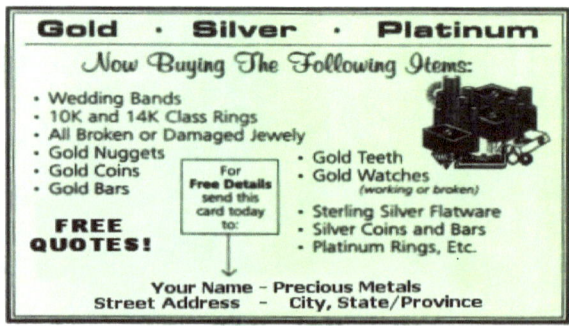

Post Card for Direct Mail Solicitations

Profiting in Precious Metals

When To Conduct Your Mailings
As stated earlier, it was a 'hit-and-miss' type of venture in the beginning. I've since refined my process so that I begin mailings in mid-October, prior to the Thanksgiving and Christmas holidays. In fact, I like to use a different postcard for this time of year, whereas I encourage the recipient to 'earn a little extra Christmas money'. This has worked for me. While I hear from men, I've noticed that it's mainly the ladies who call me asking for more details about what I am looking to buy. I assume that is because they check their mail first and my postcard is not enclosed in an envelope. That and for the most part, in my neck of the woods, it's the lady of the house who does most of the Christmas shopping. Show me someone who doesn't want a little extra spending cash for this time of year!

Web Sites
My number of inquiries increased significantly after I established an 'online presence'. I began including the address to my web site, the latter containing graphic images and detailed text outlining what I am interested in buying. I also included a form so that those individuals who prefer the anonymity of the internet would feel more comfortable in communicating with me. This increased my contact feedback by better than 30%! Just a few 'small' purchases of precious metals can pay BIG dividends!

Profiting in Precious Metals

Web Site Graphic

The above graphic was one I used successfully on a web page. The visitor desiring more information and access to the form I mentioned above, would click the 'Click Here' button to proceed. I included this graphic for a couple of reasons. First, of course, would be to give you some ideas so as to get your own creative juices flowing. The other reason being to show you what was/is successful for me. The graphic is an attention getter and after reading what is on it (which is kept brief by design), the visitor had enough information to decide if they wanted more or not.

Classifieds

Whatever you do, don't overlook the power behind the old reliable classified ad! Most, if not all communities now have some form of area publication, be it a newspaper or a newsletter. If they offer classified advertising, use it! You'll be surprised at the response that a simple text ad will produce.

Profiting in Precious Metals

Other

Of course, there are a myriad of ways to get the word out that you're in the market to buy scrap metals. The three I listed above are excellent ways plus they are easy on the pocketbook as well. However, you may be in a position that one of your relatives works at a local radio or television station and can advertise for you there at a reasonable cost. By all means, if that does happen to be the case, make use of it! That doesn't mean that you should overlook the top three mediums though. 'Pound-for-pound', they (the first three) still pack a mean *wallop* when it comes to getting the word out about your new business!

Eventually, if you stick at this for any length of time, you'll find that word-of-mouth advertising will keep you busy. Once you get a few satisfied customers under your belt, the process of telling someone about you is inevitable. Enjoy the results and smile at the price!

How to Determine What is Real and What is Not

We have all heard of 10K, 14K, 24K, etc. gold before. And most of us know that the 'K' stands for 'KARAT' or the *karat weight* of gold. But what is karat? What does the word karat signify?

Karat is the term used to specify what portion of the alloy, that makes up a piece of jewelry, etc. is *pure* gold. Think about that for just a moment. If that's what karat denotes, then it would be accurate to say that the karat weight of pure gold is 24K. By the same token, something that is only part gold, and 10 parts of another metal, would be 14K gold.

It's really pretty simple isn't it? And that simplicity is part of the beauty of this business. Once you get the hang of locating, testing, buying and selling, you'll really enjoy the freedom this business affords one. Anyway, back to the lesson.

In the business of buying scrap gold, silver, etc. you'll soon see that the vast majority of the scrap gold you pick up will be in the 10K to 14K range. 18K has picked up in popularity but the overall majority will fall within the lesser figures. Yellow dental gold will be approximately 16K.

Profiting in Precious Metals

Dental gold, however, will **not be stamped**. Just remember that the higher the karat weight, the **more pure gold** and **less other alloy** is present in a given item.

Some 'Rules of Thumb'
Items To Purchase
Any items stamped with the following numbers...

- 10K
- 12K
- 14K
- 18K

You will want to consider, and therefore, test for gold content, the following items, as well...

- **Rings** - whenever you advertise the fact that you buy scrap metal (covered in detail later), do yourself a favor and don't forget to list 'rings' among the list of things you buy. They are in abundance, from engagement rings missing stones (or those who wore them), to tongue rings, typically originating from those who outgrew them. Regardless of the type of ring, this item will prove to be a moneymaker for you.
- **Watches** - are another excellent item to consider when running your ads. Wrist watches and pocket watches are the two types you want to concern yourself with. And don't forget the metal watchbands. Some people save them, with the intention of placing it on another watch sometime in the future, only that day seems to never arrive. So much the better for you. You'll not want to skip the testing here. Many of these bands will prove to be plated but you will run across enough that are the real thing, to make it worth your while.
- **Medals, Awards, Trophies** - you will run across a *ton* of these, especially if you frequent estate sales. Such items may have been coveted by those who received them but you'll find that those who sell them, think considerably less of them. Medals will prove to be the ones you buy most often but trophies, in

Profiting in Precious Metals

particular those that originated from top corporations, can prove to be a 'diamond in the rough'.

- **Cuff Links** - you will find these in flea markets, estate sales, and individuals answering your 'Scrap Metal Wanted' ads. They're small in size but, unlike rings, they typically come in pairs. Another thing I like about this business is the fact that *small packages can reap a lot of rewards!*
- **Lodge Pins** - you will find that these are plentiful. Especially in estate sales, flea markets, etc., where it's not uncommon to find them bulked in baskets or boxes, just waiting for you to pick through.
- **Yellow Dental Gold** - I'm convinced that the *mother lode* of dental gold, remains untouched. The good news is that it will <u>always</u> remain untouched. Think about it. People save it, and what do they do with it? They throw it in a jewelry box or other equally out of the way place, and forget about it. In fact, it may go forgotten for years, until they read your ad saying that you buy scrap metal, including *dental gold*.

NOTE: Throughout this book, whenever I mention dental gold, I inevitably specify *yellow* dental gold. The reason for this is that white or silver colored dental gold can prove to be a pain to identify. Some of the white metals used by dentists are white gold or platinum-palladium alloys. I could go into further detail here and tell you why, and how these different metals can deceive you into thinking they're gold, but I won't. Suffice it to say that I personally stick to yellow dental gold and recommend that you do the same.

Items To **NOT** Purchase
Any items marked with the following...

- **G.F** - means that the item is gold-filled. For your purposes, stay away from it.
- **R.G.P.** - means the item is 'Rolled Gold Plate'. Keep your money in your pocket.
- **H.G.E.** - Heavy Gold Electroplate (need I say more?)

- **10K G.F., 14K G.F., etc.** - and a myriad of additional variations. If it doesn't say what you're looking to buy...then leave it alone.

Don't let any of the above overwhelm you. And by all means, don't try to commit every last detail to memory. It's just not necessary. If you approach this business in a simple way, you will find that it really is simple. In time, you will find that you have totally discarded all of your little detailed 'cheat sheets' (well, maybe not <u>all</u> of them) and your confidence level will soar.

If you fail to remember everything else you learn here, then do yourself a favor and do remember this. Remembering this one thing will get you out of a jam that you may not even realize you've worked your way into, and it will certainly save you some grief when it comes to your bank account.

WHEN IN DOUBT....<u>TEST!</u>

So, now you have an idea as to where and how you can obtain scrap. But how much do you pay for it? Well, this is where you must make some decisions. First, and trust me, **this is a *must***, you need to know what the day's market prices are. That's easy enough to do but if you fail to check, it could cost you some serious bucks in the long run.

In order to determine what the market is bearing, you can review the chart at the top of the gold, silver and platinum pages in this e-book. Those charts are updated daily (except weekends and holidays) and reflect what the market is doing. Visit my <u>Resources</u> page for a direct link to a site (KITCO) where the prices are displayed each day.

Ultimately, what you pay will be entirely up to you. Just do yourself a favor and remember one thing. You are in this business to make money! Believe me when I tell you that there are people out there who absolutely love to barter or haggle....and they're good at it! I say that to say this. Don't get caught up in a 'haggling war' and end up paying more than you really want to. In the end, you will regret it.

Profiting in Precious Metals

Since there are no *fixed prices* on what one should pay for their scrap, always remember to check the market charts and see what the prices are doing. Of course, you don't want to pay an amount that is so small that you get labeled as a *miser* but you also don't want to pay so much that you are tagged as a *money-tree* either! I know some buyers who pay half of what the scrap is worth and a couple who pay less than that (everything else is profit!). The best way I can assist you in this area is to provide you with an example.

EXAMPLE: A client calls me and they have a 14K wedding band in yellow gold (nothing to do with the valuation, just providing details). You weigh the ring and discover it to weigh-in at 4 pennyweights. Then, you go to your chart (at the top of the gold page or in your newspaper) and see that gold is going at $419.50 (at the time I wrote this).

Then you would open up the gold calculator and, this is where we enter into *the way I do it*, I would enter in $400.00 in the $/ounce section and click 'Calculate'. For a 14K ring, it shows that the current value (at $400.00) is $11.66 (rounded off) per pennyweight. The value of the 4 pennyweight ring is $46.64 (remember you're buying for gold content and not sentimental content!).

Once you have established a base of regular client suppliers, this part will move swiftly. They will already have an idea as to what they're going to collect. However, when dealing with a new client, who will sell you **one** ring to see how fair they get treated, you must be careful in what you say. For example, don't say "*I normally pay half of what the market reflects.*" Instead, tell them in a matter-of-fact manner "*I'll pay $23.32 for the ring.*" You'll note that's 50% of the value the calculator presented to you and actually a tad less if you lowered the markets $419.50 to $400.00 (I call this my buffer zone).

That's one example folks. The bottom line is you must know what the market is doing **that day** and if the item in question is what it is being presented as! Armed with those two all-important pieces of information, it's hard to go wrong in this business.

Profiting in Precious Metals

Now, if you're one of those yard-sale fanciers (like me - I love-em!) and you run across some items, e.g., watch-bands, lapel pins, tie-tacks and the like, and you're certain, based on the information on hand that they are indeed 10K, 14K, whathaveyou, look around and see how many they have! You don't know the number of times I've scooped up a handful (or two) of these items and paid one or two bucks!!!! These are some of my best 'lil deals' because I take'em home and chunk'em! **WHAT?!?** Did you say *chunk'em*? Yeppers, I sure did. I chunk'em....all of them....right into a rather sizeable box. After a few weeks and several yard sales or the box fills up (whichever comes first), I then take my spoils and sell them! When the quantity is significant and the quality of the items are acceptable, this can be downright profitable! Of course, you'd be wise in keeping good records of what you pay for the little items, separately from each sale. That way, you can judge if you're 'hitting the bull's-eye'!

Okay, I'm going to close the buying part of our tutorial with this. I can't provide you with every example that you'll run across and I certainly can't be there looking over your shoulder. So, remember this, if you remember nothing else. Know the market, test and pay a little. In time, the experience will just shine-forth naturally and you'll be making deals like there's no tomorrow!

Profiting in Precious Metals

Chapter 7

Selling

Once you have established yourself as a reputable buyer of precious metals, you will no doubt come to enjoy hearing from a handful of select contacts whom you've come to trust. You'll know that when you hear from them, you will walk away with quality scrap at pre-determined prices which you've set and they're content with. And that's excellent, for both you and your suppliers. A harmonious relationship where both parties leave satisfied with the outcome.

Well, the same can be said when it comes time to part with your *booty*. You'll soon find one or two buyers of your scrap whom you will automatically turn to when your *scrap chest* is full. And, just as with your suppliers, there's nothing wrong with this either. If all parties are consistently happy with the outcome of a transaction, then what more could you ask for?

Web Based 'Clip' Ad I Used

If you are fortunate, you reside in a community that is sizeable enough to have some first-rate buyers of your scrap close at hand. However, if that's not the case, don't despair by any means. It simply means that that you will probably move your merchandise through the shipping couriers as opposed to delivering it yourself. And once you get accustomed to how those transactions are carried out, e.g., how long before you can expect payment, doing so will become as easy to you as hand-deliveries are to someone else.

When I first got into this little business, I shipped my scrap stock out to a single buyer. Then, anywhere from 7 - 10 days later, I'd receive a check in the mail. This went on for a little more than a year and it worked out just fine. What that buyer paid for my scrap was quite acceptable and the slight delay in getting paid did not adversely affect me. Nowadays though, I find that I've went back to my 'roots' as far as this business is concerned, in locating local buyers who like my scrap and I like their payments....same day delivery, same day payment.

So, what do I mean by going back to my *roots*? Almost twelve years of doing this business and I find that I've gone full-circle. I sell my stock to two different jewelry businesses, both of which design and create their own jewelry, e.g., rings, bracelets, etc. One of the buyers will buy anything I walk in with that is silver. That's all he's interested in. His specialty is silver jewelry, while my other buyer will relieve me of my gold and platinum.

Pawn shops are a surprisingly good source where you can oftentimes sell your scrap. While my experience has been that they don't pay what the jewelry manufacturers will pay, I know some scrap dealers who don't hesitate in going to them. However, those dealers have told me they prefer the mom-and-pop pawn shops over the bigger franchised establishments. The smaller, independently run shops seem to offer more for the scrap than the bigger outfits. Funny, I thought it would be the other way around but that's what they tell me.

For those of you who don't have such resources readily available, you will want to check out the 'Resources' page. I've listed some companies who offer to buy your stock via mail. One word of caution here. Since I've not personally used all of the listed companies and therefore cannot vouch for their trustworthiness, I strongly suggest that you do a 'test sale' or two before sending your entire collection. By 'test sale', I simply mean that you might want to send an amount that will 'get their attention' but not break you if something goes awry. While these company names were derived from others who use them and swear by them, I simply cannot vouch for those I've not used.

Finally, you'll want to remind yourself to periodically check our *Updated Resources* link in the 'Resources' chapter of this book. Since precious metals dealers, etc. are like any other business, they come and go.

Profiting in Precious Metals

Chapter 8

Glossary

Below are some terms that are used in this business, primarily by those you will be selling to, as opposed to those you'll buy from. You may end up engaging in this business for decades and not use or hear <u>all</u> of the terms listed below. However, it's my philosophy that I would prefer sending a *soldier* out *over armed* than sending them out with just enough ammo to get themselves in a bind.

Ag - The chemical symbol for silver from the periodic tables. The symbol name is derived from the Latin word Argentum (Silver).

Alloy - The mixture of two or more metals, usually for strengthening the one which is the dominant part of the alloy. Gold is frequently (note: not always) alloyed with copper.

Ask - The price that a seller is willing to accept in order to effect a sale.

Assay - Analytic test or trial to ascertain the fineness and weight of a precious metal in coin or bullion form.

Au - The chemical symbol for gold from the periodic tables. The symbol name is derived from the Latin word Aurum (Gold).

Bid - The price offered to buy a particular precious metals item.

Bullion - Precious metal in negotiable or tradable form, such as a *bar* of gold and that are at least 99.5% pure.

DWT - An American unit of weight for gold in which one pennyweight equals 24 grains or 1/20 of a troy ounce. You will refer to it as 'pennyweight'.

Face Value - The monetary value (legal tender denomination) of a coin. This does not necessarily correspond to its actual worth. For example

Profiting in Precious Metals

the 1 oz. Gold Eagle has a face value of $50 but its real value is tied to the price of gold. **Important**: Remember that you are buying a metal for its *real value*, and not it's perceived value as a collectible, etc..

Fool's Gold - A name given to 'Pyrite' which looks like gold and has tricked prospectors throughout history.

Gram - The basic unit of weight in the metric system. 31.1033 grams = 1 troy ounce. 28.3495 grams = 1 ounce Avoirdupois.

Intrinsic Value - The actual value of the precious metal contained within an item.

Karat - A unit of measurement used to describe the purity of Gold. Pure Gold is defined as 24 Karat (sometimes spelled Carat). Common purities used in Jewelry are 10K, 14K, 18K.

London Fix - Price each day in London. Five old-line firms meet to set the price of gold and silver. This is called the "fix" and is a benchmark for market trading each day.

New York Close - Because of the time difference, the New York precious metals market continues trading for several hours after the London market has closed for the business day. Its last price has this name and it may be higher or lower than the London fix depending upon market fluctuations.

Premium - The amount over the intrinsic or "melt value" of a precious metals coin or bar.

Spot Price - The current price in the physical market for immediate delivery of the precious metal. Sometimes referred to as the cash price.

Troy Ounce - A unit of weight for precious metals. One troy ounce equals 31.1035 grams or 480 grains. One troy ounce equals 1.09711 avoirdupois ounce.

Profiting in Precious Metals

Chapter 9

Resources

Hallmarks

http://www.925-1000.com/ - they have cataloged, most, if not all silver marks that are known. An invaluable reference source.

Tools & Supplies

http://www.riogrande.com/ - one of my all-time favorite supply houses. You owe it to yourself to order their catalog.

http://www.kassoy.com/ - I've used this supplier and RioGrande with no complaints.

Buyers & Refiners

http://www.amark.com/ - This is but one place you can sell the scrap you purchase.

http://www.goldinvestment.com/ - Here is another place you can sell the scrap you purchase.

http://haroldwallacegold.com/ - Here is another place you can sell the scrap you purchase.

http://www.goldkit.com/ - Here is another place you can sell the scrap you purchase.

http://www.123preciousmetal.com/ - Here is another place you can sell the scrap you purchase or have it refined!

http://www.midwestrefineries.com/ - This is a refiner.

Updated Resources

http://www.kitco.com - This is *the site* for market prices on precious metals. They provide quotes, charts, and news about gold, silver, platinum, and other precious metals.

Profiting in Precious Metals

Chapter 10

In Closing

In closing out this reference, I thought I would add a couple of little 'surprises' if you will.

One of these surprises is FREE.

And that is, if I can ever be of assistance to you, feel free to send me an e-mail. I will eventually respond, just have patience. In the subject line, just include something like "question about testing metal" which, in your doing so, allows me to file the e-mail and subsequent response a little easier. My e-mail address is below.

gift@knightymeproductions.com

The other surprise is a FREE GIFT.

If, after reviewing my book, you find it useful in your endeavors to make money from buying and selling precious metals, please consider going to Amazon and leaving a positive review (it will really help me).

In doing so, if you leave a four or five star review and follow that up with sending me your e-mail address, using my e-mail address above, I will send you a FREE computer application that will allow you to compute the price you should pay for scrap gold, silver and platinum. It's really convenient (works well on a laptop) and very easy to use.

Thank you and I truly wish you the very best in this business! Apply what I have shared with you and have a little patience. You will not regret it!

Ron Cowart

Profiting in Precious Metals

About the Author

Ron Cowart was born in Natchez, Mississippi in 1957. In 1975, Ron relocated with his parents to Baton Rouge, Louisiana, where in 1980 he joined the Baton Rouge Police Department.

In 2011, Ron retired from the police department at the rank of Captain and now writes in his spare time.

Including this title, Ron has four books published by Amazon for the Kindle.

Profiting in Precious Metals

Hilarious One-Liners

How to Protect Your Family From Crime

Under New Management

Copyright © Ron Cowart | All Rights Reserved

www.ingramcontent.com/pod-product-compliance
Lightning Source LLC
Chambersburg PA
CBHW040925180526
45159CB00002BA/613